The Semblable:
Is a World Without
Violence Possible?

Chantal Maillard

Translated by Whitney DeVos

This is not the best of all possible worlds. Undoubtedly we can imagine better ones. The world we live in is governed by the law of hunger and the life contract we sign is embroiled in violence.

But there is another kind of violence, one that characterizes us as a species: wielded not out of necessity, but pleasure, greed, or more simply, inertia or indifference.

What will it take for us to understand that nothing is self-contained? What will it take to realize that what concerns us is much more than what safeguards us as individuals?

Take Friedrich Nietzsche, in Turin, weeping, throwing himself upon the neck of an exhausted horse that, on the verge of collapse, was barely withstanding the coachman's lashes. Biographers consider this episode to be symptomatic of the philosopher's madness. That a movement of compassion toward a non-human being is considered a symptom of insanity is a clear indication of a sick society.

If we want to recoup our health as a species, it is essential we replace the morality of reciprocity ("Do not do unto your neighbor whatever is injurious to yourself") with an ethic of interspecies compassion. To expand the framework of our belonging. Make the other, all others, human and non-human, our fellow creatures, our semblable, our *semejante*. Go from the particular to the universal. Transcend the group. Make a breakthrough.

To curtail arrogance, beliefs, false virtues, and spread global understanding and respect: Is this possible?

And, while it isn't possible for a world designed as a self-supporting organism to sustain itself without violence, can change be brought about, at least on our part, without violence?

The State of Violence
The Rules of Hunger

Usage of the term "violence" is usually limited to acts of intentional aggression. But this is a restrictive use of a word that, if we consider its etymology, simply means "abundance (*olentia*) of force (*vis*)." The state of violence is, by all outward appearances, the natural state. We are part of a world in which the rules of the game are simple: they are the rules of hunger. Those who want to continue existing have no choice but to abide by them. (Of course, continuing to exist is not the only possible option: that life is a basic good is not something that can be affirmed under any circumstances. To cease existing sometimes is, as I understand it, one of the few acts of freedom we are able to perform.) Every being survives at the expense of others. This is the primary rule. Every living being feeds on other beings, which is why any act of survival is an act of violence. Defending oneself is an act of violence as well. Both the aggressor and the victim are trying to survive, and both need to use violence in order to do so. On the other hand, we live on an unstable planet, prone to all sorts of movements. What we call "instability" is nothing but the planet's way of maintaining equilibrium. When these natural movements affect us we call them "catastrophes." We perceive their violence as an attack and respond to it by trying to defend ourselves.

But there is another type of violence that has nothing to do with survival. A gratuitous violence, exerted for pleasure, hatred, or ambition. It is this violence that distinguishes the human animal from the rest. I am not saying anything new in stating that the history of humanity or, at least, of Western society is the history of compulsive desire. This essay could easily be turned into evidence of related atrocities: it'd be enough to tack on a few convenient linkages—accounts of massacres, executions, rapes, accidents, catastrophes, torture, all sorts of crimes, current and past. Even a glance at the pictorial representations of past centuries in Europe should be enough to make us tremble. Tortures, bloody executions... Upon seeing them, one might say empathy didn't exist. Does it exist now? Back then, people were killed in public, amidst either laughter or terror, and with some god as their witness. Today, killing is (pre)recorded. There is no laughter, no god, no terror: only indifference. We contemplate news of a massacre with the same curiosity, mixed with indifference, with which we contemplate those paintings. Stories of torture also fail to affect us. We don't feel our blood run cold upon hearing them. The hair on our skin doesn't stand on end, we don't feel our flesh flinch with the memory of some hurt, of some wound. At most, a slight shake of the head or a sigh. What is the reason behind such indifference? Or is indifference our natural state of being?

What Concerns Us

I have always been amazed by the narrowness of our framework when it comes to outrage. We generally get outraged and protest only with respect to things that touch us personally. The rest doesn't seem to concern us. As if proximity and distance were ethical parameters. When what we understand to be our rights are restricted we become easily outraged, but we don't get outraged about situations in which others—who are almost always the vast majority—don't even have the right to have rights. We don't stop to think—habit is perverse company—that, in this world, some people's rights come at the cost of others' blood, and that our most minute gestures hinge upon widespread imbalances. We get outraged for certain reasons, always, but not always with good reason (justly) and, generally, not on a broad enough scale. Mostly, we defend what—or those—we understand to concern us, to affect us. We feel offended or attacked when injustice is committed against our person and its adhesions, that is, against those (beings or objects) which in some way we feel belong to us; and belongings are preserved and defended within a rather narrow framework, outside of which indifference reigns.

Much has been said about the culture of spectacle and the media's responsibility when it comes to indifference. It's true that we take in facts *cum* images like we take in fiction, through the same conduit and in the same format: that of the screen. It's also true that, in becoming news, what has happened loses its singularity. Figures are interchangeable, filed into folders with labels reading:

"migrants," "terrorists," "the abused," etc.: serialized merchandise. No singularity, reduction to (universal) concepts. Decontextualized, people become characters with no other life than the lone fragment which represents them. Of course, some images will get us to cry out, but this merely corresponds to what Kant referred to as a judgment of "taste," not a judgment of knowledge. It comes from an aestheticized emotion, not an ordinary one. Formally seduced by art's ruses, we respond to form thinking we're responding to content. This is the perversion of artistic language. Without art, on the other hand, without formal appeal, other images, holding a mirror up to the same reality, leave us indifferent. We can continue sitting calmly on the bus or in the subway while facing a poster of emaciated children. Because, beyond the possible affect the images may produce, it just so happens *we understand* that it doesn't concern us.

What does it take for something to be of our concern? Surely everyone has heard someone else exclaim, in front of the television screen, "I know that person…" Or "That place is around the corner, I was just there this morning!" And you must have noticed a certain inflection in the voice, as if something had suddenly taken its toll—and seen the person examine the screen with greater interest, as if looking for something familiar, something that could build a bridge between the external and the internal… All of a sudden, she was concerned.

The main reason for our indifference, those of us who partake in societal "well-being," is that the violence (that our nations carry out) always occurs Elsewhere: on distant shores or, simply, the basement of the neighboring building. Violence occurs Elsewhere, but is exerted globally.

Global Violence / Global Outrage / Global Nausea

We all know or are aware that banks have our accounts at their disposal as a means to finance the arms industry. What we don't know, of course, is which bullet or antipersonnel mine will explode thanks to our savings account or who will be the victim, but we can imagine in which regions it will take place. Or we should, being that global violence, itself a violation of territories without territory, in fact concerns us. There are no borders in this game; the limits are others or there are none. Global violence is not a war but a dirty game in which there are those who dictate the rules on one side of the board and, on the other, pawns. Corrupt governments with puppet rulers, deals fixed among elites, secret societies without any visible leaders, population displacements, blackmail, misappropriations, undue expropriations, massacres... The universe of the global market is no longer Kafka's castle, but a very well organized business, and the consequences, for millions of beings, are neither Kafkaesque nor virtual; they are simply real. A reality imposed upon the flesh, with pain, with exhaustion. And we are involved in all of it, whether we want to be or not. Our nations and governments are, our economy is. But all this is obvious, certainly, and you will tell me, not without reason, that what we have to do—us philosophers—is not so much to think about it as to think from it. However, I think even knowing this, we risk losing sight of reality as it stands. Thinking about a financial crisis without thinking about the gears of consumer society, thinking about local outrage and its immediate causes without thinking about the global reasons behind it, doesn't strike me as being logically sound, or ethically correct.

So I return to the question: What will it take for us to feel that all of this is of our concern? To avoid indifference? For us to care that what we do here has its repercussions on the Other Side? We grow, we feed, we "make progress" atop heaps of corpses, over and above the misery and suffering of entire peoples, human and non-human, who are foreign, alien to us. And we aren't outraged by it. We don't go out into the streets to protest the fact that our companies displace entire populations who resist the establishment of factories and the stealing of their land, nor because agribusiness corporations relentlessly torture millions of animals in farms and slaughterhouses.

I know these things are uncomfortable. We don't like to be made to feel guilty. "It wasn't me..." "What can I do about it?" or also, "Now isn't the right time, with everything we're dealing with right now...." But shouldn't we first ask ourselves what is going on and why? We can't let pressing issues be the reason we lose sight of others, because "others" are the context of what is in close proximity and if we don't remedy the context, what we do with what is in close proximity will be of little use. In other words, nothing is self-contained. Only a global vision and global outrage will be able to stop global violence, the disaster it entails; or mitigate the global nausea it produces and, in its place, foster local actions that revert, if not into well-being, into better conditions on a global scale.

Perhaps indifference is caused, as someone once wrote, by the sheer complexity of relationships in a globalized world which has ruptured the link between our actions and their consequences. Perhaps our imagination and our actions have become out of step, rendering us "incapable of imagining their consequences and, therefore, of being morally responsible for them."[1] Maybe that's it. When complexity increases past a certain point, like Descartes' ten-thousand-sided polyhedron, things become impossible to imagine. Or, more simply put, this generalized desensitization arises from the difficulty we have, in global society, of establishing the relationship between our economy—from which we derive the series of quotidian gestures that, taken together, constitute our way of life—and the horrors endured by other beings Elsewhere.

It is time to awaken. Today, outrage cannot be limited to defending one's private interests. Because, yes: for everyone, it is a matter of surviving, only some of us/we continue to live at the expense of others who barely survive.

The Semblable

I have used the verb "to awaken." This makes me feel a bit messianic, which bothers me. "It is time to awaken," I said. And I would already be regretting saying it if it weren't for the words of Derrida that now come to mind: "The *unrecognizable* is the awakening." This phrase belongs to the

Seminar *The Beast and the Sovereign*, where the author responds to a comment made by Lacan[2] with respect to cruelty. What is typical of cruelty, according to Lacan, is that the human being always targets a semblable, even when he directs that cruelty toward a being of another species. The fraternalism of the semblable, Derrida believes,[3] frees us from any ethical obligation, the duty not to be criminal and cruel to any living being who is not my "fellow" (semblable) or who isn't recognized as such.

And, certainly, if we look back, we would see that taking up a defensive position vis-à-vis unlikeness (difference, dissimilarity, otherness, *dissemblable*) is how European nations were able to justify the genocide of the Amerindian populations as much as the enslavement of Africans or, until not very long ago, the subjugation of women. And, even now, it's also by sheltering ourselves in dissimilarity that societies of the written word allow ourselves to displace, steal, and reduce to misery those people without a written language, from whose survival strategies we could learn, if only we lent them our ears and attention. Yet, on the contrary, they are silenced.

Derrida puts it like this:

> A principle of ethics, or more radically of justice, in the most difficult sense, which I have attempted to oppose to right, to distinguish from right, is perhaps the obligation that engages my responsibility with respect to the most dissimilar [*le plus dissemblable*, the least "fellow-like"], the entirely other, precisely, the monstrously other, the unrecognizable other. The *"unrecognizable"* [...] *is the beginning of ethics*, of the Law,

> and not of the human. So long as there is recognizability and the fellow, ethics is dormant. It is sleeping a dogmatic slumber. So long as it remains human, among *men*, ethics remains dogmatic, narcissistic, and not yet thinking. [...] *The "unrecognizable" is the awakening.* It is what awakens, the very experience of being awake. The "unrecognizable," and therefore the non-fellow [*le dissemblable*]. If one trusts and binds oneself to a Law that refers us only to the similar, the fellow, and defines the criminal or cruel transgression only in what it is targeting as fellow, that means, correlatively, that one has obligations only to the fellow [...]. More obligation toward men than toward animals, more obligation toward men who are close and similar than toward the less close and less similar (in the order of probabilities and supposed or fantasized resemblances or similarities: family, nation, race, culture, religion). One will say this is a fact (but can a fact ground and justify an ethics?): it is a fact that I feel, in this order, more obligations toward those who closely share my life, my people, my family, the French, the Europeans, those who speak my language or share my culture, etc. *But this fact will never have founded a right, an ethics, a politics.*[4]

That it is in fact so does not mean it should be so. The moral of the "fellow" (*semblable*) rather seems to arise in order to justify the radical fact that, in defending my "fellow neighbors"—that is, those I am close to, those who get close to me—I am defending my surrounding circle, I am defending myself. This, in effect, does not found an ethic, nor does it correspond to an ideal of justice. Because justice, in an ethical sense, transcends group legitimacy.

Lacan's concept, according to Derrida, leads not only to all forms of racism, but also to one being able to inflict the worst sort of suffering upon an animal without being suspected of the slightest cruelty. There is no "crime against animality," he says, nor is there a crime of genocide as far as non-human living things are concerned. And as for good intentions, they are loaded with anthropocentric naïveté.

> As for the declarations of the rights of animals called for by some people, beyond the fact that they never go so far as to condemn all putting to death, they most often follow, very naïvely, an existing right, the rights of man adapted by analogy to animals. Now these rights of man are in a relation of solidarity and dissociability, systematically dependent on a philosophy of the subject of a Cartesian or a Kantian type, which is the very philosophy in the name of which the animal is reduced to the status of a machine without reason and without personhood.[5]

It is no doubt comforting to discover a philosopher in whose speech one feels a sense of refuge (even if he has, as is the case, not a few detractors). Above all, because we have reached that point where one usually perceives, somewhere in the auditorium, a condescending smile partially suppressed at the corners of someone's lips. We don't all agree. Because: "This is irrelevant, here, in this forum, where serious things are being seriously discussed." It is curious how one can feel important when taking a stance about things that are supposed to be important. "How are we going to think about animal abuse or glaciers melting when there are so many millions of unemployed in this country?"

Yes, the "semblable" is taken seriously. The "other" is not.

Is ethics something that only works in boom times, and is cast aside whenever we feel we are in danger?

Thinking in such a way is like seeing wildfire growing closer and focusing on the fortification of one's own lair. No, as much as we try to defend our possessions, we won't escape disaster. Because nothing is self-contained. Taking care of the social group we belong to, taking care of the flock and its territory, of course this has to be done, but starting with a broader sense of awareness. If we strive to preserve our national and professional interests to the detriment of world and planetary interests, we'll do nothing more than slap a patch on a raft that, sooner or later, is bound to sink.

Laughter Is a Defensive Weapon

In certain parts of the world, those of us who speak publicly about animal rights still do so, it must be said, with a certain fear of ridicule, fear that we'll be found guilty of a terrible violation of logic, morality, and common sense: How can we possibly equate animals to humans?

Laughter, gentlemen, is a defensive weapon. A vestigial gesture of baring the teeth, as Darwin put it. One ridicules in order to neutralize, to avoid some sort of damage, some breach in the walls. Why is the human individual offended when equated with an animal? Because he considers them inferior. Inferiority is an extremely useful notion: it justifies utilization and even extermination. Until recently,

Westerners considered people of other ethnicities inferior. Andean peoples were not human beings (as it was decreed in Valladolid in the middle of the sixteenth century), and African slaves of the Americas did not have souls. Nor did certain women have them, until well into the nineteenth century. And although having a soul may seem quite irrelevant to some, the fact is it made a difference significant enough to obviate a sector of the population from being considered "subject," that is, a "semblable," a being with self-awareness that no one may attack or abuse without being charged. (Remember: according to the ethos of the semblable, there is no cruelty or criminality except as against one's fellow.) The "soul" was something as necessary for capitalism (and, prior to that, being so for the ecclesiastical estate) as the phlogiston was for seventeenth century science, or the invisible substance for the medieval Aristotelians who condemned Galileo.[6]

Inferiority is a conceptual requirement for domination, and is upheld by a series of comparisons. In the case of animals, these were established in the West according to the biblical mandate "Go forth and multiply; fill the earth and subdue it." (Of course, Genesis was written by a man and not by a horse, as Kundera put it.) Comparative justifications were formulated *ad hoc*, like the existence of the phlogiston, in order to prove something that had been decreed in advance. Since then, the likeness or unlikeness which validates our appreciation or contempt for an animal continues to be measured according to unquestionable and unquestionably anthropocentric values (whether or not the animal is capable of laughing, or playing, or pretending to pretend, whether an ape can perform mathematical operations, whether an elephant takes pleasure in painting, whether the whistle of the dolphin is identitarian, whether the DNA of the vinegar fly differs very much at all from that of the human... Well! An interesting observation has crept in here!) that point to the identity-subject the human individual claims distinguishes him. Proof that an animal is aware of itself would render it worthy of respect and perhaps even deserving of certain rights. Because to be self-aware is to be a subject, and without a subject there exists no right that is valid. The "semblable," once again.

The issue, in reality, is not so much the obvious naïveté with which we establish these types of comparisons as the schema that asks us to establish them: a hierarchical, bifocal, and infantile schema, above and below, superior-inferior. We undoubtedly have a strange propensity for verticality. There are other ways, however, to proceed. Other models may be considered, in which one does not proceed either by derivation (evolutionism) or by comparison and equivalences (structuralism). Within a truly ethical (not moral) framework, respect is not obtained according to the place one occupies (a higher degree of it, the closer you are to the top), but rather by the fact of simply being what one is.

The Narrowness of the Framework

I can't help but be surprised at the small scale of our framework of outrage. The virtues of the animal lost in me I admire very much, and I deplore very much the macabre inclinations of the human animal and the lack of coherence of a rationality that, having logic (and therefore justice) as its foundation, strives to protect at all costs its own species to the detriment of others and, consequently, of its own. I don't feel superior to any being for being part of a species that has developed its intellectual capacity at the expense of the systemic notion that appertains to all animals.

Nothing is self-contained. A species cannot be destroyed without the entire chain suffering the consequences and, when this happens, the survival of the human species is also jeopardized. Unfortunately, for many people human survival is the only reason we should care about the planet at all, and the only reason that those of us who talk about it don't have to suffer the sight of shrugged shoulders or complacent smiles. Speciesism that points to the bounded enclosure of our territory and tips the implementation of justice toward the meagre pan on our side of the scale. That's how narrow our framework is.[7]

Would the meaning of equity become too broad if it were to imply that the right to life, liberty, and territory for survival is not exclusive to the human being?

The ancient formula of reciprocity, "Do not do *to others* what you do not want done unto you," which so many traditions share, could be rethought from the ethic of the semblable since, well, who are "others"? Both the Talmud and the Book of Tobias are about other men, of course. Confucius was very explicit about it: "What you do not want done to you, do not do to *other men*."[8] The Buddha's ethic, on the other hand, was more comprehensive: *"All living beings* desire happiness. They all fear death. Comparing ourselves to others, we should refrain from hurting or killing." Could it be that Buddhism doesn't think within the parameters of logical equivalence? No, it is still an equivalence, only here likeness is measured not by attending to the face (that face capable of *responding*, as Derrida would say) but something more radical: the condemnation of dying, and the fear of suffering and of death.

Having been born, having appeared, having fallen into time, for a time, from the abyss of non-life, deserves, given the suffering all this in fact implies, the respect of *"morituri te salutant."* And the additional suffering that, in human beings, derives from the ability to anticipate irremediable decline, aware of its *befalling*, the fall itself, and their rejection of it, doesn't make us more worthy of respect than any other being; it just makes us more wretched.

And, What Can We Do?
Facing the Feeling of Impotence

The first obstacle, for those interested in posing this question, as I have pointed out before, is that we don't concern ourselves with anything other than what pertains to us most directly, that part of the whole (family, group, country, nation, or species) to which we feel we belong. Of primary importance, then, is to foster an extension of the membership framework. This is a foray into the field of rationality, certainly, given that it has to do with logical equivalence, but a rationality guided by a broader principle.

Above all, it's important to understand that what we do here has its repercussions all over the world, that nothing is self-contained, and that only a global vision and global outrage can put a stop to global violence and the disaster it entails, by fomenting actions that result if not in well-being, at least in a better state for all. This involves knowing how to position ourselves in such a way so as to understand the place we occupy in the chain and know how to distance ourselves enough from our particular interests so as to be able to direct action toward a common good. This implies transcending moral equivalence ("Do not do unto your *neighbor*—he who is similar to you—what you would not want done to yourself"). The question can no longer be posed in terms of people or likeness; the moral of the semblable is that of us–others, of "us" before "others," above "others," and, if necessary, against "others." The moral of the semblable is that of differences understood not from a rational point of view (of justice, of equivalence) but a biological one: defense of the clan in the name of protecting its members. But, I'll put it in the words of Susan Sontag: You shouldn't be assuming a "we" when it comes to the pain of others. The common good must be considered rationally at the global level, and so must the action aimed at restoring equilibrium.

The difficulties inherent in all of this will escape no one. The first of these is the obsolete model of thought we continue to draw on. Despite the fact that quantum theory is now over a century old, we still think that difference must be ordered following the schema of the Porphyrian tree. We don't seem to have realized that there is another way of thinking about matter (the famous *substance* of the philosophers), that there exist other logics which make it possible to understand that nothing "is" once and for all, that the universe is a continuum of being and that, in order to continue being, any one thing depends on all the others.

The second difficulty is that the perspectives created by capitalist ideology make it difficult for us to comprehend that the current economic system is not the only one possible. In this way we become a docile flock, too well-off to have reason enough for a radical change, a *revolutio*.

The third difficulty is the degradation of the democratic system, that is, the one through which we should be able to elect people to make decisions that would bring about change. We've had plenty of opportunities to ascertain that our sainted democracy is not the ideal system they led us to believe it was. Rather, democracy is something more akin to "that great narrative of the West in whose name, in order to secure perpetual and definitive peace in the world, they have taken and have undertaken international police operations of the bloodiest sort."[9] Democracy has become synonymous with pantomime (from the Greek *pantomimos*, "actor," literally "imitator of all"; *panto-* meaning "all," and *mimos*, "imitator" or "actor") since electoral candidates are actors subservient to capitalist interests. Electoral candidates are actors. (Is it only by chance that some of the governors and presidents of the United States have been Hollywood actors?) On the one hand, the people, the *demos*, never govern, among other things because the "People" does not exist; it's a concept. What does exist: spectators who will applaud and vote for whoever best performs his or her role and masters the art of representation.

Government by majority would be a good system only if its majority were capable of self-directed reasoning, which is not the case; and even if it were, if the majority were to contemplate the possibility of not delegating important decisions—which isn't viable when the number of individuals is numerous. The majority does not tend to think particularly well. If they did, they would understand that the good candidates are the ones who stay out of the pantomime, receiving neither votes nor applause. On the other hand, those who are elected, as soon as they are, wherever they come from, become part of something called Government, a concept in opposition to that of the People. And the point is that, when Government and Capital shake hands, there doesn't seem to be any means left for managing resources according to the principle of rationality: that is, of equity. The change, then, has to come from other places: we must arrive at the principle of rationality together, despite or against the system. Clearly the need for change is essential. But can we avoid violence? Is nonviolence an option?

Ahiṃsā. **Nonviolence as a Political Action**

It is commonly believed Gandhi invented the concept of nonviolence. Nothing could be more incorrect: the *ahiṃsā* can be traced back to the origins of the Upanishad tradition, and to the precepts of coexistence in some of the oldest religious communities in India. What can be attributed to Gandhi is the political use of nonviolence as a form of resistance to political domination. An active use which, together with the concept of civil disobedience, thus transforms the negative formula *a-hiṃsā* ("no harm," "no aggression") into a political act. This was, in fact, quite a deft tactic designed to provoke moral outrage not only among the Indian population but also among the other nations of the world. It was accomplished by the end of the Salt March (1930) when, following instruction from Gandhi himself, protesters allowed themselves to be beaten to death. The intent was not to avoid bloodshed, but rather to render martyrs of some and immoral dominators of others in everyone else's eyes. "Perhaps no one understood so precisely the essential role that moral outrage could play in a political conflict," writes the sociologist Losurdo in a reference to Gandhi.[10]

The oldest citation of the word ahiṃsā is probably the one in the Chandogya Upanishad, a reference to the compensation of priests.[11] But it's also one of the four vows that were observed in ascetic communities and the first of the ethical norms (nonviolence, truthfulness, honesty, chastity, and detachment) the yogi must observe in the first stage of his learning, just as Patañjali would recount in the subsequent systematization of this method. Of the many religious communities which proliferated around the sixth to fifth centuries BCE, only Buddhism and Jainism took on historical dimensions, and the practice of nonviolence is fundamental in both. Jainism derives from a very old ascetic tradition. Its unification dates back to Mahavira, a contemporary of the Buddha Shakyamuni (late fifth century BCE).[12] For the Jainist, the ahiṃsā is the most important vow; in the case of the ascetic, it's extended to mean any type of violence; in the case of the layman, the vow is limited to intentional violence: since, by being in the world, one cannot avoid action and since all action entails some kind of violence, accidental, occupational, and protective violence are tolerated in the secular world. The ancient *sāṃkhya* system, from which Jainism adopts its cosmology, understands living beings as interconnected, interdependent monads and, therefore, responsible to one another; hence the necessity to avoid harming any other being. "Do not do unto others what you do not want for yourself" is also a Jainist maxim.

For both Semitic and Indo-European peoples of antiquity, logical equivalence soon acquired a moral character. We find it in the Talmud, in the Old Testament, in the Mahabharata (XIII, 115, 22) and in the Buddha's sermons. But Confucius also prescribed it in his *Analects*. Here, it's a matter of the practical application of a universal law that conceives of the "mean" as the center in which opposites are reconciled. The "mean" is the point at which equality is possible because it is the germ of mutations: that point at which transformations haven't yet begun. Where there are no differences, there is equality. Whoever understands the principle of equality does not go up against others, but instead treats them how he would like to be treated, Confucius thought. He who stands outside the "mean" starts a war; he who knows how to place himself within the "mean" is a man of peace. From this principle of equality is derived both the formulation of the maxim "what you do not want done unto you, do not do unto other men" and the preeminent role, in Confucian morality, of the virtue of humanity (*jen*), which originates in the rational intuition of the fundamental non-difference between forms of the living.[13]

In Buddhism, nonviolence does not find its origins in the principle of equality, as in Confucianism, nor in the law of reciprocity and interdependence, as in Jainism, but in the principle of compassion. "All living beings desire happiness," said the Buddha, "all fear death. Comparing ourselves to others, we should refrain from hurting or killing." Compassion (*cum-passio*: "suffer-with") derives, in Buddhism, from the awareness that suffering is the condition shared by all living beings. The ascertainment of existence as suffering (duḥkha) is the starting point of the path, and also part of its end: the *bodhisattva* (the "awakened," "enlightened," or more literally, "the one with a lucid mind") is the one who compassionately decides to stay among the living in order to continue teaching the way. In this case, nonviolence is not a principle but a collateral consequence of this insight.

One cannot conclude on the basis of these movements, their existence notwithstanding, that the history of the Indian subcontinent has been a peaceful one. This isn't at all the case; it wasn't at the start, and it isn't now. Let's not forget that Jainism and Buddhism were the two great heterodoxies of Hinduism, both dissident movements undesirable for Brahmanic society, whose literary references are no less bloody than the Bible's. Let's keep in mind that, just as justice isn't necessary where there is no injustice or benevolence where there is no bad faith, neither is it necessary to speak of peace (or nonviolence) where there is no state of violence. The Vedas are not peaceful books. The Aryans were conquering nomads. In the Atharva Veda, we find hymns for conquering enemies (VIII.8). In the Rig Veda, Indra is called the "punisher of guilt" and, as for the epics, neither the Ramayana nor the Mahabharata are any more peaceful than the Old Testament or the *Odyssey*. Furthermore:

the first great reference text of Hinduism, the Bhagavad Gita (part of the Mahabharata), constitutes a defense of legitimate violence in order to combat injustice, even if it's specified this violence has to be employed in an unbiased way, with a spirit of equanimity, without any personal interest in the results, out of duty alone. And therein lies the trap, of course, since, just as in Kantian ethics, the question is: who dictates duty?

Since Gandhi, nonviolence has been understood in a manner rather distinct from the Jainist concept which implies not doing harm to any being. It is, in the political domain, the use of one force to counteract another. That public acts of nonviolence are a political weapon is something current governments are very clear about. Without going any further, in Spain, in the face of peaceful protests of 15-M, in 2011, the Ministry of the Interior decided to modify the penal code to equate passive resistance, until then considered a "crime of disobedience," with "assault on authority." Passive resistance was, in the words of then-Secretary of State Security Ignacio Ulloa, "conduct equivalent to aggression committed against the principle of order and authority exercised by security forces and organizations."[14] And it is true that we accept all too easily the fact that state violence is legitimized violence. Minority violence, on the other hand, is never legitimate; it is "destabilizing."

When democracy has been degraded and nonviolent struggle (a contradiction *in terminis*) or passive resistance are considered aggressions, what can be done? While it is clear that there is no possibility of a world without violence, is it possible, at least, for change to take place without violence?

Five Notes for a Deactivation Program

I. In Singular

It's always been my understanding that sociopolitical reform doesn't yield lasting results, unless it is begun with individual consciousness-raising. Because concepts do not exist. What exists exists in the singular. It's in the singular that one suffers, in the singular one is afraid and in the singular one endures dissatisfaction and the pangs of unsated desire. Change will have to be achieved by all of us together, but its potential needs to take shape in each person, one by one, since internal knowledge isn't something that can be obtained in the plural; it's up to each individual. And this knowledge is the condition of possibility such that the change, if it does take place, is not simply one more dialectical oscillation, but a radical one.

At this crossroads, I suggest starting our reflection over in the singular. Pain always occurs in the singular. And so it is from this point that solutions must be sought as well: not from the top down, but with the personal work of each of us.

No system will be successful unless we learn to apply the principle of rationality within a broader framework. We must gain an understanding of our place of belonging. Understood correctly, "property," what is "ours," is not what we possess, but the place to which we belong. What is needed is a habitat wisdom, an *ecosophy*: a wisdom (*sophía*) of one's own (*oikos*). *Eco-sophy* instead of *eco-logy*, wisdom instead of discourse. Habitat wisdom is knowing that nothing is self-contained, that we are a speck in the universe, the same as a spider, a rhino, a plant, or an amoeba. The wisdom of the *oikos* entails decreasing in importance so as to place ourselves in our corresponding place within the great entanglement of the living.

Lay down false beliefs. Reject anthropocentric values, inherited opinions and (re)cognition. Remove the residues. Unlearn in order to recover prior knowledge blinded by discourse. *Dis-courses*: sediments that, in abundance, hinder the course. Laozi had this in mind when he spoke of the loss of the tao:

> The *tao* lost, virtue [*te*: strength, virtue] began to act. *Te* lost, compassion [*jen*] replaced it. Compassion lost, justice was resorted to. Justice, too, was lost, and became substituted by courtesy. But courtesy is not particularly loyal or trustworthy, and is the beginning of unrest. The science or knowledge of such virtues is just the flower of the *tao* and the beginning of stupidity.

Could humanity, with its exalted wisdom and false virtues, find the resolve to go back to that which these sought to replace?

II. An Education in Sentiment

I've never been able to help noticing that we're able to stare at terrible events on a screen while having lunch. That we turn on the television at the same time every day to watch the newscasts knowing (and, above all else, we know) we'll probably be told about some tragedy, that under the pretext of "being informed," we'll be able to partake in violence and continue eating. What strange power is this, that of representation, which leads us to pleasurably experience sensations that in real life would cause us grief, pain, terror, or disgust? What sort of pleasure is this? Because evidently it's about pleasure, isn't it?

In 1757, the Irish philosopher Edmund Burke stated that if, within a crowded theater about to show the play of the moment, word suddenly spread that a criminal was going to be executed in the plaza, the theater would promptly empty out. Burke thought the human disposition to contemplate the misfortunes of others was due to a wave of *sympathy*—a word that in Greek literally means compassion—a feeling which is pleasurable, since it derives from love and social affection. Is this the case? Is it out of sympathy, or out of compassion, that the spectators leave the theater and rush to the square, where the scaffold was being prepared? Because they would, wouldn't they?

Thirty years after Edmund Burke spoke so naïvely in this regard, the people of Paris flocked to the Place de la Concorde, then called the Place de la Révolution, to watch with relish as heads rolled into a basket waiting at the foot of the guillotine. This device, by the way, wasn't particularly beloved by the public, given that it significantly shortened the duration of the show. More than eleven thousand public beheadings took place during the French Revolution, much to the citizens' delight. Was it sympathy and compassion that brought them to the plaza?

Is it out of sympathy or compassion that audience ratings for daytime soaps drop when newscasts cover a plane crash?

Rome and its circuses are not such a long way off. It's true that sacrificial rites eventually became symbolic and that, from gladiator fights, we moved on to soccer, a "civilized" variant of the spectacle, but perhaps this is precisely why we need to see blood flow in virtual form. But why do we derive pleasure from it?

It's not really the fact of seeing others die; it's not the violence itself from which we derive pleasure. Nor is it, as some philosophers have thought, the relief we may feel in becoming aware that we're safe, by comparison, nor that any passions, even painful ones, are preferable to tedium. What gives us pleasure is representation. And there will be representation whenever we position ourselves as spectators.

Broadening the framework of belonging demands we know how to neutralize images of *world-representation*, the effect of which keeps reality at a remove from our "own" life. Disarticulating the associated pleasure mechanism which accompanies it involves knowing how to distinguish between ordinary and spectacularized emotions. All emotion is capable of being aestheticized when the factors of representation intervene. One of them is the distance at which we position ourselves when we become spectators. In front of a stage or screen, the ordinary subject automatically becomes a spectator subject, establishing the distance that allows him to empathize, in a non-ordinary way, with the added pleasure the staging affords him.

Pleasure is a plus which accompanies any emotion, regardless of whether it is pleasant or unpleasant in and of itself.

Dramatized, ordinary emotions like grief, fear, or disgust are transformed into pleasurable emotions. The specific genres (drama, horror, or gore, among others) which led to the film industry are proof of this.

Since time immemorial, representation has been the simplest way to educate people in certain values. *To educate* means "to drive" or "direct" (*ex-ducere*) and one lets oneself be directed easily if there's pleasure in it. The issue, then, is our being able to de-*art*iculate the *art*ifact. The point is, on the one hand, to learn to recognize this pleasure and distinguish it from emotion in its pure state; and, on the other, to separate the content of the images from the scenic and/or aesthetic effects.

Emotional pleasure is not the only kind of pleasure involved in representation. There's also the pleasure of the "as if." The "as if" creates the space of fiction: a space full of tension between the "is" and the "is-not," between what's real and what isn't. All representation is a metaphor, following the same schema: "it is (as if it were) what it represents, but it is not." The pleasure of metaphor is a pleasure of the intellect. The more distantly the two terms are related to one another, the more tension there is between the is and the is-not, and the greater the pleasure experienced by the imagination when putting them into play and substituting the one for the other. Intelligence likes surprises. They sharpen it.

The pleasure of the "as if" is derived, on the other hand, intuitively, like with the metaphor. A comparison in which the grammatical particle "like" is omitted, there are no grounds for judgment. Thus, the representation is received immediately as (if it were) what it represents without us needing to become aware of the deception.

When we position ourselves as spectators, we're ready to receive what happens in the tension-filled space of the "as if," where the real appears *as if* it were fiction and fiction *as if* it were real. If the public goes to the public square to attend the execution of an accused, it's because the square has been transformed into a fictional space and the individuals have become spectators. The plaza is a stage and what happens, a show.

Screens themselves provide a fictional space. Like public plazas, screens are stages: squares or quadrilaterals in which the game takes place. All we have to do is reposition ourselves, from ordinary subjects to spectators, for the performance to begin.

We are all familiar with the perils of "bad art"; we should recognize that art is much more dangerous when it's good. When skillfully utilized, the arts can be and are a form of applied politics. And since politics is now (and when hasn't it been?) a market economy, markets now utilize the arts to craft consumerist values. The problem, for those who partake of their product, will be to find out who they serve, for what purposes and with what values. This is also a condition *sine qua non*, moreover, for any artist who seeks to wield the renovative function of art: the *per-version* or reconversion of an order that is established to the detriment of liberties.

It's urgent we educate ourselves about emotional discernment. We typically lack the historical perspective necessary for acknowledging the epochal sentimentality by which we operate, or notice the vested interests which promote it. Forms of sentimentality are not, in effect, spontaneously generated, but cultivated. The "basic emotions," as they were once called in India, give rise to many variants which belong, strictly speaking, to a specific time period and culture: the sublime, for example, is characteristic of romanticism, sentimentality of the early twenties, tedium and boredom date back to WWII, and kitsch, which appeared in tandem with industrialization, is reaching unprecedented heights, today, to the market's great benefit.

In societies in decline, emotional modalities become degraded, it's a fact. But today degradation is an instrument of globalization in the hands of the leisure industry. If we examine, for example, the Hollywood remakes of certain Japanese horror movies, we see how they turn *pathos* into a simple neuro-vegetative reaction. It's about frightening instead of terrifying (terror being the aesthetic category of tragedy). Walter Salles' remake of *Dark Water*, the splendid film of the same title directed by Hideo Nakata just three years earlier, is a quintessential example. In the version released in the United States, there is an evident lack of key devices crucial to getting to the root of fear and representing it effectively. Resorting to sound effects instead of subtly dealing with the mind's associative qualities demonstrates a lack of understanding as to the origins of emotions, which the artist must be intimately familiar with in order to be able to express them effectively, so that the whole experience may then be resolved into a higher-order understanding.

Instead, however, the originals are simplified in Salles' film so as to offer a readily-grasped explanation. Above all, it's about the spectator regaining composure at the end, making it important to eliminate all former traces of discomfort. Any derivation toward the absurd or the nonsense of agreed-upon responses is dangerous: thinking is not suitable for individuals. The spectacle must serve to numb them. Hollywood is a strategic machine in service of Capital, and its purpose is maintaining the mental health of the enslaved. Catharsis is nothing more than that: an implosion lasting only as long as the show's climax, well-measured and directed toward the restoration of mental and moral composure by a script upheld by the socially-accepted moral code.

I'm not going to suggest anything new in saying the time has come for the spectator to take responsibility for himself as such. He must be able to recognize when he is being manipulated and how. He must be able to identify music and separate it from the ideas being conveyed, in films as in political life. He must be able to observe in himself where emotions are produced, what kind they are and what prompted them. We have to be mature spectators, capable of distinguishing when a work has indoctrinating intentions and of what kind. These are questions Brecht thought carefully about; and he did not limit himself to just thinking them, but he put in place a theatrical mechanism in order to do so. Did he succeed? I have the suspicion that his approach was swallowed up by the needs of the theater: those of the spectator, of being engrossed in the action; those of the actor, of engrossing the spectator; and those of the stage, being after all: a stage, a fictional space. The paradox of the Brechtian proposal is that, in this way, the theater continued to be a space for educating and its theatrical content, pedagogy.

The question is the following: is it possible to attend to the means of representation without losing empathy? Is it possible to be conscious of fiction and, simultaneously, allow ourselves to be overcome by it? To be critic and spectator simultaneously, making judgments and submitting to experience?

An attentive spectator can tell when he is being manipulated by what he sees and how. To do this, he has to know how to distinguish everything that pleases him (music, forms, clothing, colors) at first sight, and separate all this from the ideas conveyed by the images. But, above all, he must be able to observe within himself how his emotions are engendered, what kind they are and what triggers them. In short, he must know how to distinguish *senti-mental* movements from the pleasure accompanying them, which is produced by the effects of representation. Is it possible to remain conscious of a fictional plot while under its influence? Is it possible to be observer and spectator at the same time?

III. The Banyan of Howrah

In a place known as Howrah, about fifteen kilometers east of Calcutta, there is a banyan tree, over two hundred and thirty years old, with a surface area covering about fourteen thousand five hundred square meters. At the top, its circumference reaches almost a kilometer. Despite currently living without its original trunk, which had to be cut down, the tree continues to grow.

This type of Bengal fig or *ficus benghalensis* grows horizontally; its branches put out aerial roots that dig into the ground, forming what—at first glance—look like trunks.

What would happen if, instead of designing the world in accordance with the Porphyrian tree, as has been done so far, we were to take the Great Banyan tree as a model? What would be entailed in a paradigm shift of this sort?

The Porphyrian tree is a conceptual tree. It refers to a diagram used in medieval texts to illustrate the classification of substance as it was understood by the philosopher Porphyry (c. 232-304 CE), disciple and biographer of Plotinus. This system of classification was the one used during the Middle Ages, and its model has been followed in all sorts of subsequent efforts at taxonomy. The schema follows a template in which concepts are vertically distributed, from the abstract concept of "substance" to that of "man"—leaving out, of course, everything that does not serve this definition. This schema served as the starting point for the development of European thought and, subsequently, the technology of the Western world.

The Porphyrian tree is a vertical, hierarchical, exclusive, patriarchal, logical model, which proceeds with expressly constructed dichotomies: substance (corporeal or incorporeal), body (animate or inanimate), living (sensitive or insensitive), animal (rational or irrational), rational (man). The banyan tree, on the other hand, is a living tree. Its aerial root system expands into the air and below the ground, tracing between them an uninterrupted circuit.

Two ways of understanding the world. The model of patriarchal rationalism, which thinks in terms of the Porphyrian tree: vertically, brushing aside everything except what is in its own interest. And the model of matriarchal populations, wherein thinking happens in terms of correlations, horizontally: a mother trunk whose horizontal branches send out roots that anchor into the ground, the action or movement of each part coordinated with the others—what we call "environment" or "surroundings," when we think about ourselves using anthropocentric values. Mineral sap: as alive as those beings we consider alive, in contradistinction to others. Roots that are trunks, interconnected, all of the same status.

Status, yes, because that is what it's about, an order of importance. Social articulation responds to the linguistic model: in terms of verticality, the universal, whether called a concept or aristocracy, will be positioned at the top and the particular, the simple extant realities or the proletariat, below.

Replace this model with a horizontal, inclusive model, in which all individuals (human and non-human) have the same status, even if the mother trunk disappears. Think and act in terms of subsistence and universal respect rather than in terms of production and profit. Build a living reality according to a horizontal model not in the service of compulsive desire, greed, or power but the mutual sustenance of species… Does this make sense?

The universe is a network in which everything we do or fail to do has repercussions. This is what was never grasped by rationalistic and patriarchal individualism.

IV. Aesthetic Reason

Over two decades ago, with optimism stemming from having a body still intact, and on the basis of the idea that the human species is something in and of itself valuable, which we consider to be a good one without having evaluated it, I came up with the practice of aesthetic reason.[15] It was not about emotional reason, nor was it about merging, as some did, after Nietzsche, reason and life as if they were one thing and its opposite. No: reason is not the opposite of life. Reason is an instrument for life. Our mistake was to convert that instrument into an overarching category and, in that way, lose our ability to perceive ourselves as belonging to the organism of nature and our ability to conduct ourselves in accordance with its rules. It was therefore a matter of returning logos to its place and of recovering what had been forgotten: channels of perception obstructed by judgment.

Aesthetic reason purported to be a perceptual, sensory consciousness (*aisthesis* means "sensation" in Greek), capable of attending to flow and seeing reality not as an amalgam of separate entities, but as a happening along-with. If the verb "to be" were to be replaced by the verb "to happen," many things would change. Opinions would be relativized, and the need to establish truths would be replaced by the need to create spaces of coherence in which to build necessary fictions: stories one does not need to believe, since they belong to the order of aesthetics, not to the order of logic, and that, therefore, would not be a source of conflict.

At least that's what I thought. Though it was undoubtedly due to the optimism that comes with childbearing age, when the body is still willing to cooperate in perpetuating the survival of its species—and of itself.

○

I crumble a eucalyptus leaf between my fingers; I breathe in its scent. I crush a sprig of rosemary; its pungent smell seeps into my arteries. Everything vegetal within me seems to awaken from the depths of the prior and something like photosynthesis takes place in my body as it comes into contact with light, bright and clear. No, we are not different. For the good of the species, we multiply in times of adversity even more than in prosperous times, just like plants. To ensure ourselves a place on the planet. So it, too, survives. Order, limits, extinctions, appearances, all of this is dictated from without—or from within, however you look at it—by the consciousness of that plural organism all of us make up together.

It would not be illogical to think that violence between human groups contributes to the self-regulation of the biological planetary organism. The species' own internal violence diminishes a populace which, having no natural predators, endangers the rest of the planet. Unlike other animals, it seems we have lost our sense of the collective instinct regulating the system. But on the other hand, there is no doubt that a reason capable of considering the situation with greater sense of equity exists in opposition to the individual will to survive, since, obviously, no one wants to disappear.

Will there be some means of bringing individual will and theoretical reason into agreement? I don't know. As far as I am concerned, it's clear to me that if nature, needing to restore equilibrium, attacked me, at no point while defending myself and fighting for my life, as any animal would do, would my capacity to reason allow me to stop to think that, in all fairness, losing the battle would be the right thing to do.

V. From the Morality of Reciprocity to the Ethics of Compassion

In order to mitigate what's to come, be it change or eventual defeat, and avoid the surfeit of violence our avaricious nature begets, it's in our interest, above all, to expand our notion of what is *of our concern*. Because, if there is something in which all beings are alike, apart from hunger (in any of its forms), it's the suffering this violence entails.

That Friedrich Nietzsche's embrace of an exhausted, mistreated horse was considered a symptom of madness indicates how sick the society in which we live actually is. We have prioritized reason, its capacity for speech and analysis, over any other type of intelligence. And we have exerted reason to the point of allowing the atrophy of other forms of immediate knowledge, those that put every animal in relation to habitat and prevent behavior from undermining the equilibrium of the system upon which we all depend. This previous intelligence was called "instinct" and was despised, in that way depriving us of an indispensable tool.

The human animal, the most recent arrival, and the least evolved. Poor creature who, unable to understand any language other than its own, had to turn human language into a distinguishing feature of a superiority that, in truth, he can only claim when it comes to the sheer scale of human stupidity, ignorance, violence, and the capacity to destroy. Being more evolved does not mean being superior; it just means having arrived last. That a higher order of neural complexity should give us the right to grant ourselves a post of greater planetary relevance only demonstrates how readily we extrapolate mathematical values to the purview of the ontological and ethical whenever it is convenient for us.

To *alien-ate* ourselves would be desirable: to extend the framework of belonging, to go from the adjacent to the alien, to breach borders. *Dis-integrating* into others, protecting difference, knowing that, along with the natural violence it brings about, is the way in which the universe perpetuates itself. This would deepen our lucidity—and common sense.

In order to do this, first and foremost we must modify our perspective. Acquire global vision.

Second, we must curtail compulsive desire. Calm down. Want less. Need less. Dismantle our system of consumption by controlling the compulsive desire at its roots.

Then, invert patriarchal values (growth, progress, profit) and replace them with subsistence values. Decrease. Distribute. Restore equilibrium. There are options. The current system isn't the only possible system and it's certainly not the best.

Decrease in all senses of the word. Become aware of our plague dimension. Decrease in species pride and willingness to endure above all. Temper the fear that makes us desire immortality. Become aware of the transience all existence implies.

And, finally, expand the horizons of the principle of rationality. To justice (equivalency), add understanding; to intelligence, wisdom. Replace the moral of reciprocity with the sense of compassion.

A utopian program, it doesn't escape me. Seen from scientific parameters, clearly naïve. Insufficient, of course. But it's a starting point. And, given prevailing scientific naïveté, a balancing factor.

May we remember Friedrich Nietzsche in Turin, clinging to the neck of a horse, crying out for forgiveness for humanity; and, in that way reversing, with a universally compassionate gesture, the hierarchical order which places the human being at the top of a pyramid manufactured *ex professo*. May the day soon come when that episode is considered lucidity of the highest order.

References

1 Eduardo Romero, *Quién invade a quién. Del colonialismo al II Plan África* [Who Invades Whom: From Colonialism to the Strategic Plan] (Cambalache: Oviedo, 2011), 19.

2 Jacques Lacan, *Écrits*, (Paris: Seuil, 1966), 125–149; trans. Bruce Fink as *Écrits: The First Complete Edition in English* (New York: Norton, 2006), 102–122. In Jacques Derrida, *The Beast and the Sovereign* Vol. 1., trans. Geoffrey Bennington (Chicago and London: University of Chicago Press), 97.

3 Derrida, *The Beast and the Sovereign*, 107.

4 Ibid., 108–109. Emphasis added.

5 Ibid., 110–111.

6 "'The moon is not a perfect sphere,' Galileo asserted. 'Mountains and craters can be seen on its surface. See for yourself,' he says to his adversaries, holding the telescope up for them to see. 'Okay,' they answer, 'but there is an invisible substance that fills up the craters, making the moon spherical. A spherical substance…' 'Very well,' Galileo answers, 'but that substance does not fill up the craters; it is piled on the top of the mountains, making them even higher than can be observed, and the craters even deeper.'" A.F. Chalmers, *What Is This Thing Called Science?*, third edition (Indianapolis/Cambridge: Hackett Publishing, Inc., 1999), 76–77.

7 It should be clear that affirming the superiority of the human over other beings is not typical of all cultures; it is, primarily, a feature of the technocratic individual who, having ceased to put his *tekné* in service of survival, puts it in service of profit. This is what distinguishes fundamentally agrarian societies, based on the principle of subsistence, from those based on the principle of productivity. The Western, patriarchal concept of nature as resource—exploitable, productive, inferior and domitable—is inseparable from the Judeo-Christian tradition.

8 *Analects* IV, 5; XII, 2; XV, 23.

9 Domenico Losurdo, *La cultura de la no violencia* [The Culture of Nonviolence] (Barcelona: Península, 2011), 16.

10 Ibid., 122.

11 "Austerity, charity, righteousness, nonviolence and truthfulness: these are the priest's honoraria (*dakṣiṇā*)." (Chandogya Upanishad, 3.17, 4)

12 Mahavira was not the first teacher of this tradition, nor would he be the last. Trying to locate the founder of any tradition reveals the adoption of a strictly Western historicism. "The Indian sage generally does not found, or invent, or create, or write; rather he remembers..." Agustín Pániker, *Jainism: History, Society, Philosophy and Practice*, trans. David Sutcliffe (New Delhi: Motilal Banarsidass, 2010), 137.

13 *Analects* IV, 5; XII, 2; XV, 23.

14 Público.es, 20.04.2012.

15 Chantal Maillard, *La razón estética* [Aesthetic Reason] (Barcelona: Galaxia Gutenberg, 2017).

Translator's Note

Chantal Maillard's *El semejante* is a text which thinks alongside the Lacanian concept of *semblable* as outlined in *Écrits*, as well as Derrida's reading of Lacan in *The Beast and the Sovereign*. The French term *semblable* (Spanish, *semejante*), for which there is no English equivalent, has been translated into English in different ways in psychoanalytic literature ("fellow," "counterpart," etc.), none of which capture the dual connotations of the word as both adjective ("similarity/likeness") and noun ("fellow creature, fellow man"). A footnote from the English translator of *Écrits*, Bruce Fink, on existing translations of *semblable* helps to illuminate the various possibilities one has at hand when translating the original Lacanian term into English:

> Lacan's term *semblable* is sometimes translated as "fellow man" or "counterpart," but in Lacan's usage it refers specifically to the mirroring of two imaginary others (a and a') who resemble each other (or at least see themselves in each other). "Fellow man" corresponds well to the French *prochain*, points to man (not woman), the adult (not the child), and suggests fellowship, whereas in Lacan's work *semblable* evokes rivalry and jealousy first and foremost. "Counterpart" suggests parallel hierarchical structures within which the two people take on similar symbolic roles, as in "The chief financial officer's counterpart in his company's foreign acquisition target was Mr. Juppé, the *directeur financier*." Jacques Allen-Miller (in a personal communication) has suggested the translation "alter ego" for *semblable*, but since "alter ego" is also occasionally used independently by Lacan and since it has a number of inapposite connotations in English ("a trusted friend" and "the opposite side of one's personality"), I have preferred to revive the obsolete English "semblable" found, for example, in

> *Hamlet*, act 5, scene 2, line 124: "[H]is semblable is his mirror; and who else would trace him, his umbrage, nothing more."*

For the reasons he outlines above, Fink goes with the obsolete "semblable," in usage in English during Shakespeare's time (and, which, according to the *OED*, enjoyed a revival in the twentieth century, perhaps due in no small part to T.S. Eliot's citation of Baudelaire in *The Waste Land*: "You! hypocrite lecteur!—mon semblable,—mon frère!"). Derrida's translator, Geoffrey Bennington, opts for "fellow," however. Because Maillard quotes directly from Spanish translations of *Écrits* and *The Beast and the Sovereign*, and requested citation of the existing English translations, I had to do some shuttling between the different terminology used by Fink and Bennington. In translating *El semejante* I've chosen to introduce Lacan's concept as "semblable" (following Fink), while treating Derrida's handling of this same term as "fellow" (as it appears in Bennington's existing English translation). Maillard's unique, interspecies rendering of the concept (*el semejante*) appears as the "ethic of the semblable."

As is the case with semblable in both English and French, the Spanish *semejante* is, in its noun form, a synonym for *prójimo* ("neighbor," "fellow human"); *prójimo* is the word used in the Bible, particularly in Leviticus 19:18, for which the common English phrasing is "you shall love your neighbor as yourself." When Maillard refers to *la ética del semejante* ("the ethic of the semblable") she does so not only as a Derridian trace of *The Beast and the Sovereign* but also—and above all—in contrast to Judeo-Christian morality, which is the foundation of the West's

---

* In *Lacan to the Letter: Reading* Écrits *Closely*, (Minneapolis: University of Minnesota Press, 2004), 169.

anthropocentric societies, and which refers exclusively to those who belong to the same categorical group, i.e. equals, fellows, the closely-related, kin, neighbors: *prójimo*.

An important aspect of Maillard's text involves a Derridian language game using variations on the verb *cercarse* ("to come close, gather around, surround, fence in, enclose") and the noun *cerco*, a term that can mean "frame" or "fence," as in a barrier, boundary, enclosure; *cerco* can also refer to a siege. On page 10, Maillard draws out the restrictive sense of enclosure one's implied by one's surrounding community, which itself is by implication separate from other possible communities; in this instance, I have translated *cerco* using the colloquial phrase of "surrounding circle" which touches on several, though not all, of these aspects: proximity; a close-knit group; and being surrounded. On page 15, *cerco* is used to denote a bounded territory and appears simply as "enclosure." The word's first appearance in the text, however, is significantly more difficult to translate. When it comes to Maillard's call to "*romper el cerco*" on page 1, we must concede that English lacks the adequate resources for conveying the multi-faceted meanings of *cerco*, only one of which is "frame" whose Spanish equivalent, *marco* ("frame," "framework"), is itself a governing metaphor throughout *The Semblable*. I've rendered "*romper el cerco*" as "make a breakthrough" to suggest, if indirectly, its affinity with notions of abolishing borders (political, physical, ontological, categorical), breaking cycles, and expanding the frameworks of our outrage, ideas which resonate throughout the text.

Maillard, a specialist in the philosophy and religion of India, frequently engages with precepts such as *duḥkha* (suffering), itself a product of *taṇhā* (thirst, desire, longing, greed). One possible translation of *taṇhā* in Spanish is *ansia*, which can refer to both anxiety and agitation, as well as a longing, desire, or craving that is often, but not always, inflected by connotations of greed, appetite, and gluttony. *Ansia* is used, for example, to communicate "a yearning for freedom," "a thirst for knowledge," or "the lust for power." An important concept in Maillard's greater body of work, *ansia* is "the great contemporary perversion"[*] in so far as desire drives the market and, hence, both capitalism and consumption. *Ansia*, which for Maillard is "associated with the myth of progress and happiness," I have translated throughout as "compulsive desire."

Finally, a note on political context. On page 23, Maillard makes passing reference to Movimiento 15-M (*movimiento de los indignados*, "movement of the outraged"), an anti-austerity movement in Spain that began in May 2011. 15-M arose in response to consequences of the Great Recession, and the consequent lack of political alternatives to the conservative Partido Popular. Taking form as a series of protests, demonstrations, strikes, and occupations, 15-M influenced other similar movements, including: Occupy Wall St. (United States, September 2011); YoSoy132 (Mexico, May 2012); and Nuit debout (France, March 2016). 15-M continues to exist in a residual form.

—*Whitney DeVos, October 2020*

---

[*] See Maillard's interview with Javier Rodríguez Marcos: *El País*, 2/20/2020 (https://elpais.com/elpais/2020/02/19/ideas/1582131992_494785.html).

The Semblable
Copyright © Chantal Maillard, 2020
Translation Copyright © Whitney DeVos, 2020
Adapted by the author from the book *¿Es posible un mundo sin violencia?* [Is a World Without Violence Possible?] (Editorial Vaso Roto, 2018).

2020 Pamphlet Series
ISBN 978-1-946433-67-1
First Edition, First Printing
Edition of 1,000

Ugly Duckling Presse
The Old American Can Factory
232 Third Street, #E-303
Brooklyn, NY 11215
uglyducklingpresse.org

Distributed in the USA by SPD/Small Press Distribution
Distributed in the UK by Inpress Books

Series design by chuck kuan and Sarah Lawson
Typeset by Don't Look Now!
Type is New Century Schoolbook
Cover paper and flyleaf from French Paper Co.
Printed offset and bound at McNaughton & Gunn
Flyleaf printed letterpress at Ugly Duckling Presse

This publication is made possible, in part, by support from the New York State Council on the Arts, a state agency. This project is supported by the Robert Rauschenberg Foundation.

 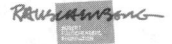

This pamphlet is part of UDP's 2020 Pamphlet Series: twenty commissioned essays on poetics, translation, performance, collective work, pedagogy, and small press publishing. The authors are listed below; their pamphlets are available for individual purchase and as a subscription (uglyducklingpresse.org/subscribe). Each offers a different approach to the pamphlet as a form of working in the present, an engagement at once sustained and ephemeral.

Mirene Arsanios
Omar Berrada*
Sergio Chejfec
Don Mee Choi
Kunci Study Forum & Collective
Iris Cushing
Simon Cutts
Nicole Cecilia Delgado
Adjua Gargi Nzinga Greaves
Dimitra Ioannou

Sibyl Kempson
Claudia La Rocco
Aditi Machado
Chantal Maillard
Tinashe Mushakavanhu
Sawako Nakayasu
Tammy Nguyen
Aleksandr Skidan
Steven Zultanski
Magdalena Zurawski

*Nadine George-Graves & Okwui Okpokwasili

To win a subscription, write to office@uglyducklingpresse.org with your solution to the following puzzle: Using only 6 straight lines divide the circle on the back cover so that each number is in its own section, without any overlap between numbers.